Meditation

Attaining A Profound Mental State And Attaining Profound Relaxation, Alleviation Of Stress, And Diminishment Of Anxiety Through The Practices Of Yoga Nidra And Yogic Sleep

Khalid Burt

TABLE OF CONTENT

Mastering The Basics Grounding 1

Contemplation And The Means Of Acquiring It? 11

Our Ancestors Understood The 29

The Significance Of Meditation And Prayer 29

Transcendental Meditation 58

Mitigating Discomfort And Minimizing Distractions Exercise 73

Types Of Meditation 77

By Means Of The Virtue Of Forgiveness, Tranquility 86

Considering The Options Available For Fulfilling The Requirement 104

Powerful Meditation Tips 117

Tackling Fear 150

Mastering The Basics Grounding

Assume a comfortable seated position with your feet resting on the floor. From my experience, I have found that utilizing an exercise ball as a seating option offers the utmost comfort, as it promotes proper spinal alignment while allowing my feet to rest comfortably on the floor. However, it is important to note that alternative seating arrangements, such as assuming the half-lotus position or sitting on a conventional chair, may be more preferable to some individuals.

Regardless of the seating arrangement you opt for, ensure that you can sustain this position comfortably for an extended period if your intention is to engage in meditation subsequent to grounding. Transitioning from one position to another has the potential to disrupt the tranquility that has been cultivated in one's mind.

After you have settled in and become at ease, kindly shut your eyes and initiate a series of unhurried, profound inhalations. Inhale via your nasal passage, ensuring a duration of either 3 or 4 counts, then proceed to exhale through your oral cavity, maintaining a similar count of 3 or 4. While inhaling, take cognizance of the gradual influx of air into your lungs, and upon exhalation, observe how your abdominal region expands and contracts correspondingly.

Whilst inhaling, conceive a notion of pristine, untainted energy permeating your physique, and upon exhaling, envision the expulsion of any detrimental thoughts and energy, such as stress and apprehension, from within you. Continue to do this for several minutes until you feel calm.

Once you feel prepared, commence the process of visualizing your feet possessing elongated roots, resembling those of a tree, and firmly embedded within the depths of the earth. Initially, it may be necessary for one to engage in the process of envisioning these roots. However, through the passage of time and dedicated effort, an individual will gradually cultivate a heightened consciousness of their existence.

Just as trees and plants absorb moisture from the ground through their roots, envision the innate energy of the Earth ascending into your body.

Elevate the energy by starting from your right foot and perceive its ascent along your right side, ultimately reaching the pinnacle of your head. As it commences its descent along the left side of your body, visualize it effortlessly expelling any residual negative energies that may continue to reside within you. The energy descends into the earth via your left foot and subsequently travels inward through your right foot, maintaining an uninterrupted and consistent flow.

You are now subject to a restriction on your activities and have acquired the rudimentary skills of meditation.

Opening the Chakras

In order to access and activate your chakras, it is imperative that you possess a thorough understanding and retention of their sequential arrangement along with their corresponding hues. (Initially, if you find it challenging to recall all of them, you need not be overly concerned.

It may be helpful to jot them down on a sheet of paper and position it within your line of sight as a point of reference prior to commencing.)

Utilizing the existing energy flow within your body, begin redirecting it towards the base chakra.

Once more, the utilization of visualization techniques will assist you in accomplishing this task. You will be required to perceive the chakra. In my personal sentiment, I envision it as a blossom that remains sealed; however, feel free to select the metaphor that resonates with you. Certain individuals envision it as a lusterless crystalline substance that gradually intensifies in luminosity.

Observe the energy as it flows towards the chakra, infusing and saturating it. Concurrently, witness the gradual unfurling of the red flower bud, its petals gracefully expanding until it attains complete blossoming. After it has become opened, permit the energy to proceed unabated along a direct, upward trajectory towards the sacral chakra. Employ the identical procedure across all the chakras, altering the hue of the flower accordingly as you progress.

Upon the opening of the crown chakra, you will be presented with two alternatives.

It is possible to redirect the energy in such a manner that it returns to your left foot, thereby maintaining the initial circuitous flow.

OR

One may release the energy by emanating it from the crown of the head and enabling it to gracefully envelop one's entire being. Subsequently, the unbroken stream will ascend through the space between your legs, traversing the chakra pathway and exiting through the crown of your head. This will create a defensive enclosure around you during the time when your chakras are open. The objective of this practice is to maintain the containment of untainted energy within oneself and prevent the infiltration of any negative influences.

If you desire to purify your chakras, now presents an opportune moment to proceed. Visualize a spigot at the location where the energy is being introduced into your physical being. For a brief duration, intensify the energy from a consistent flow to a torrential current.

As your skills in this area develop, you will observe a noticeable enhancement in your perception of your spiritual self. You will gradually develop the ability to discern which chakras are obstructed or experiencing mild congestion. Once a blockage has been identified, it is advisable to dedicate additional time towards harmonizing the energy within the respective chakra in order to achieve complete clearance.

Closing your Chakras

The act of closing your chakras holds equal significance to that of opening them. It is not advisable to completely deactivate them, as doing so would result in a cessation of the energy flow. Your objective is to maintain a slight opening of the flower in order to allow a gradual flow of energy.

This procedure mirrors the reversal of the chakras opening process. Initiate the process by directing your attention towards the crown chakra, visualizing the influx of energy permeating its essence, and subsequently gradually diminishing the aperture of the floral representation until only a faint stream of energy remains coursing within it. Descend to your Third Eye chakra and proceed with the replication of the aforementioned procedure. Descend further towards the base chakra.

Whenever you commence the activation of your chakras, it is imperative to observe and follow the subsequent sequence for their closure. When one maintains an open state of their chakras while navigating the course of daily existence, it is highly probable that they will experience profound exhaustion. Whether through depleting one's own energy or, as frequently occurs, someone else sapping it on one's behalf.

Although many individuals may not realize that they are depleting your energy, there are those who are acutely aware of the extent to which you are being drained and will exploit it.

Contemplation And The Means Of Acquiring It?

Transcendental Meditation exemplifies highly effective techniques for meditative practice.

Transcendental meditation has breathed fresh vitality and renewed significance into one of the countless age-old practices of meditation. This practice can be traced back to the ancient Vedic tradition of India, which occupies a central position in the field of studying human consciousness and unveiling its inherent potentialities. The Vedas are the oldest human religious culture.

Maharishi Mahesh Yogi, renowned physicist and philosopher, unveiled this method of meditation to the public. Initially, it was exclusively accessible to a select group of individuals. Over the course of the last two and a half decades, Maharishi has facilitated the training of numerous instructors in the art of meditation. The global proliferation of transcendental meditation has given rise to a novel comprehension of the practice. This meditation technique can be easily acquired and is applicable to a wide range of individuals. It necessitates minimal prerequisites, as it is not contingent upon any specific lifestyle and is devoid of any inherent affiliation with political or religious customs. This phenomenon is rooted in established principles of the mind and body, exemplified by the aspiration to enhance one's well-being. The prime aspect of its influence lies in its avoidance of tedium. This becomes apparent shortly after attaining mastery of the skill. Numerous individuals hold the belief that attaining a meditative state, characterized by disregarding incessant thoughts and experiencing spiritual serenity, is an unattainable goal for them. The Transcendental Meditation technique harnesses the innate psychological inclination to transcend ordinary thinking, in order to minimize the exacerbation of issues caused by prevailing thought patterns. Meditation bears resemblance to the act of submersion. The subject of proper entry into the water during diving training has been addressed by American psychiatrist, Bloomfield, who states that it is crucial to possess the skill of gracefully descending into the water. If the diver descends into the water perpendicular to the surface, all subsequent actions follow naturally as a result of gravitational forces. It is imperative to place one's trust in the force of gravity. During the practice of meditation, the mind returns to its fundamental mode of thinking, analogous to how an individual in a dimly lit room instinctively gravitates toward the source of light. "

The "immersion process" is facilitated by three key factors: first and foremost, assuming a comfortable and stationary sitting position; secondly, closing one's eyes; and finally, carefully selecting an object of meditation. To facilitate the liberation of the mind from the relentless cycle of daily concerns and to foster a gradual decrease in mental exertion, mantras are utilized as an invaluable resource. The term "mantra" originates from Sanskrit, the venerable classical language of ancient India. The term originates from the etymological derivation of the word 'man', denoting 'cognition', combined with the suffix 'tra', which connotes the capacity for practical implementation. Therefore, the concept can be described as "cognitive instruments" or "means of cognitive facilitation." By utilizing mantras that do not induce strain, the meditative process initiates. The mantras employed in transcendental meditation elicit a regulating and calming influence, devoid of any drowsiness-inducing properties. The effects of their impact, as substantiated by a multitude of scientific studies, possess characteristics that uniquely facilitate cognitive stimulation.

Your focus and receptivity during the practice of Transcendental Meditation are heightened. It is unnecessary to direct attention towards the object of meditation. On the other hand, the process of immersion should transpire inherently and reflexively. Concentration prevents self-absorption.

If one desires to acquire the knowledge of transcendental meditation, it can be accomplished under the guidance and tutelage of professionally trained instructors. They will consider your unique aptitude for acquiring knowledge and effectively elucidating the various meditative encounters. Additionally, based on my personal observations, they possess a comprehensive understanding of numerous meditation practices.

Nevertheless, it is imperative to acknowledge that meditation has not been exclusively devised by any singular individual or collective. It is not related to any religious practices. It is not required to partake in initiation rites for this purpose. It may be argued that it would be best if no one were to instruct you in the practice of meditation. Guidance can be beneficial, although not essential. Indeed, the practice of meditation can be easily attained by individuals of all backgrounds with minimal exertion. As previously mentioned, the capacity to engage in meditation is innate within each of us by nature. In every modality of meditation, individuals endeavor to attain a state of tranquility and intra-personal communion. If one exhibits diligence and sincerity, the desired outcome will invariably be realized.

When to Meditate?

Allocate a dedicated period for the practice of meditation early in the morning, if possible, prior to consuming breakfast. Engaging in meditation will provide you with the necessary fortitude and vigor to sustain optimal productivity throughout the course of the day. Subsequently, designate an equivalent duration during the evening, ensuring a minimum interval of four hours prior to retiring for the night, as this will facilitate a natural recuperation process following the session.

If you engage in meditation during late hours, it can disrupt your sleep patterns due to the concentration required on the designated topic. Nevertheless, certain individuals opt for the practice of soothing and tranquil meditation sessions in close proximity to their bedtime. Evening meditation aids in the elimination of detrimental emotions amassed throughout the course of the day.

To achieve optimal outcomes, it is imperative to consistently abide by a predetermined timetable. Engaging in daily meditation is more beneficial than meditating twice a day or practicing meditation every other day. It is imperative to strive for a cumulative impact. The length of the training period is a crucial determinant in attaining optimal outcomes.

Indeed, mankind continually engages in contemplation. This is a perpetual endeavor. It is an indispensable aspect of existence, akin to the essentiality of air, without which individuals who fail to engage in it purposefully and proficiently experience a stifling deprivation of vitality, much like an insufficiency of oxygen. After embarking on a meditative practice, your being will undergo a transformative process from which there is no return. The objective is to incorporate meditation into your daily existence.

It is important to acknowledge that within several established meditation programs, there exists a significant lack of success among participants. The vast majority of individuals who partake in these courses (which typically carry a hefty price tag of several hundreds of dollars) initially exhibit a fervent allegiance to the practice of meditation. However, subsequent to a few weeks or months, their frequency of meditation diminishes and eventually ceases altogether. If you have made the decision to incorporate meditation into your daily routine, I would advise you to prioritize it from the outset by allocating specific time for it in your daily activities while setting other obligations aside. Please refrain from asserting that you lack the time. It is necessary for you to locate it. If one engages in occasional meditation, the outcomes are diminished.

What is the recommended duration for my meditation sessions?

Meditation sessions are recommended to have a duration of approximately fifteen to twenty minutes. While a strict framework is not present, it has been noted that this approach yields optimal results.

Through the practice of meditation, an enhanced sense of well-being will gradually manifest. Consequently, you will find yourself inclined towards engaging in meditation for an extended duration beyond what is strictly required. However, just like in any other circumstances of your life, it is imperative that you exercise rational judgment. Excessive duration of meditation is not considered a commendable quality.

The objective of meditation lies in establishing a connection with one's reservoir of inner strength, drawing inspiration, and seeking internal guidance, rather than solely focusing on attaining elevated states of consciousness.

Where should I meditate?

I hold the opinion that it would be beneficial for you to primarily engage in meditation within the confines of your home. Seek out an appropriate setting for solitude, ideally a room adorned with ambient lighting. It is imperative for it to be shielded from any external auditory disturbances. The presence of noise impedes the attainment of conscious awareness and hinders the ability to concentrate and establish a connection with the Universal Mind.

It is advisable to engage in daily meditation at a consistent location. Over time, a sense of positive energy becomes established, fostering a state of relaxation. This location will inherently evoke feelings of serenity and tranquility.

Pose

An ideal posture is achieved when the spine is maintained in a straight position, supported by the backbone, while ensuring complete relaxation of all other muscles. This requirement is most comprehensively fulfilled in three traditional meditation postures, assumed on the ground:

1) Seated in the cross-legged position, commonly referred to as "Turkish style".

2) Adopting a kneeling posture;

3) "Lotus".

The aforementioned are the benefits inherent in adhering to the classical poses. The act of assuming a seated position on a chair or stool during the practice of meditation may engender apprehension or perhaps an irrational fear of entering into a state of deep absorption, thereby impeding the progression of the meditative process. The flooring additionally instills a perception of safety. The pose of sitting on the floor with legs crossed is likely to be the most suitable for the majority of beginners. Occasionally, this method is referred to as "an ergonomic stance."

Sitting in this manner is incredibly pleasant, and in various eastern nations, this posture is prevalent in everyday routines. If one intends to engage in meditation while assuming this posture, it is crucial to ensure that the head, neck, and spine maintain a seamless alignment.

Where should one position their hands? There are two options. One possible alternative in a formal tone could be: "The initial position involves placing the palms onto the knees." It would be advisable to commence with this suggestion. In the second iteration, typically applicable following the attainment of a certain level of meditative expertise, it is advised to adopt a posture wherein the hands are interlaced akin to the shape of two receptacles placed one within the other. According to Indian customs, the right arm is positioned at the bottom, while the left arm is positioned at the top.

Individuals who favor their left hand - the reverse. The thumbs should rest gently against each other, simulating the act of completing the circuit.

The second traditional position for engaging in meditation - assuming a posture with the buttocks resting on the heels. In order to accomplish this, it is necessary to assume a kneeling position with the knees firmly pressed together, ensuring that the toes remain parallel and the heels are slightly apart. Please assume a seated position with your heels resting on the floor. The cranial region, cervical region, and thoracic region align in a linear fashion.

This particular stance is widely observed/distributed/adopted across

Japan. In this particular setting, individuals engage in more than just meditative activities; they also partake in pursuits such as writing, reading, eating, and engaging in other tasks while assuming this posture. Whilst the Japanese have been accustomed to assuming this posture since childhood, many of us, especially those with well-developed thigh muscles, may initially find sitting in this manner uncomfortable. To acquire proficiency in this posture, it is recommended to proceed at an exceptionally gradual pace. It may induce discomfort in the musculoskeletal system temporarily, hence it is advisable to first attain proficiency in assuming the crossed-legged position.

Lotus Pose, a fundamental yoga asana, is particularly conducive to contemplative practices such as meditation. Depending solely on the hip and knee joints to sustain an erect posture entails a minimal expenditure of energy. Assuming a lotus position requires minimal effort as it entails complete absence of muscular strain, thus facilitating undivided focus.

Nevertheless, attaining proficiency in the "Lotus" pose can be a challenging endeavor. Nevertheless, through diligent and intentional practice, it can be accomplished. It is not advisable to engage in such activities beyond the age of 50 years. I would like to underscore that the attainment of expertise in the lotus position should not be treated as a sole objective. Meditation primarily entails mindfulness rather than physical prowess. Accomplished meditation can be attained through various positions beyond acrobatic poses.

Our Ancestors Understood The

The Significance Of Meditation And Prayer

It is my contention that in the era of slavery, our forebears resorted to employing public prayer as a method to discreetly transmit coded messages, thereby facilitating communication and organization. They could engage in clandestine discussions and strategize their emancipation. Others were under the impression that they were engaging in a spiritual practice.

The slave owners deprived them of all channels of communication; however, our predecessors resorted to rhythmically tapping their feet, applauding their hands, and vocalizing in sync with the cadence of a drum. In the present era, it is commonly referred to as Morse code. The African clergyman would engage in rhythmic sermons and supplications. The initial connotation associated with the art of communication as freedom fighters has become obscured and is presently unappreciated.

I recall the character Belle, the wife of Kunta Kinte, in the historical film "Roots" discussing a recent addition to the plantation with their daughter, Kizzy, using the phrase "He belongs to a distinct category of individuals." "He is unaware of his origins." In essence, she was implying that he possesses no knowledge of his personal history, resulting in a state of mental disorientation. He had adopted the mindset of subjugation that his oppressor intended to cultivate within him. He found himself immersed in a culture that obscured his perception, leading him to acquiesce to the circumstances of his existence as an inherent entitlement. Our forebears possessed a higher degree of spirituality, surpassing that of the individuals who enslaved them and identified themselves as followers of Christianity.

Upon the release of "Roots," I witnessed a distinguished clergyman express the belief that the greatest benefaction slavery bestowed upon the Black community was the introduction of Jesus Christ. While I acknowledged this statement, it failed to resonate with my inner being and caused profound uneasiness within my core. I maintained my silence as a sign of reverence towards the preacher. Subsequently, I gained insight into the process by which the preacher reconciled the aforementioned concept within the framework of their religious doctrine. During my formative years, an annual initiative was undertaken in numerous communities with the purpose of collecting funds for the acquisition of Bibles. These cherished books were intended for distribution in African regions, aiding in the spiritual enlightenment of individuals who had not yet embraced Christianity, as they were encouraged to embrace the teachings of Jesus Christ and proclaim him as their divine savior. That was the deeply ingrained dietary mindset that resided within the individual who frequently possessed a high level of education and made diligent efforts towards advancing the emancipation of the African-American community.

As I matured, I gradually recognized that our forebears possessed a profound comprehension of the Christ principle of love and the more profound, hidden aspects of "pure" Christianity, which are intricately ingrained in ancient Kemet through hieroglyphics inscribed in stone. The preceding generations coexisted in accordance with the profound doctrines espoused by Jesus, comprehending the fundamental premise that "God is a Spirit and ought to be venerated with sincerity and genuine devotion," well ahead of the rise of papal authority in Rome, the reign of King Herod, and the reign of Pilate.

Based on the findings of Dr. Yosef Ben-Jochannan, it can be inferred that the foundational principles of various significant religions were derived from African origins. Reverend Dr. Ruben Green, my esteemed college professor at LeMoyne-Owen College, extensively discussed the renowned scholar Dr. Yosef Ben-Jochannan in our esteemed academic courses of World Religion, New Testament, and Philosophy. In his lectures, Dr. Green acquainted us with the mythology surrounding Ausar (Osiris), Aset (Isis), and Heru (Horus).

While I was enrolled in seminary, the professor of church history astounded me with their knowledge and insights. During the initial two classes, I attentively absorbed the lecture content, simultaneously contemplating the forthcoming discussion on church history and pondering the purpose behind exploring this particular topic. I had been anticipating news regarding the arrival of Jesus in Bethlehem. It quickly became apparent that he had already commenced the class. I experienced a sense of satisfaction and contentment throughout my presence in the class, and I harbored a deep appreciation for the opportunity to partake in the course.

The professor delved extensively into the subject matter of the course, imparting knowledge supported by scholarly references. The inception of his exploration can be traced back to ancient times, as he delved into topics such as Ancient Kemet, Nubians, Kush, Africa, Egypt, Tehuti, Imhotep, Akhenaton, Nefertiti, Aset (Isis), Ausar (Osiris), and Heru (Horus), Hatshepsut, Cleopatra, Thutmose, and various other figures. He rearticulated the information that was conveyed by Dr. Green during our academic pursuit of the "Survey of Biblical Literature" module at LeMoyne-Owen College. According to the testimonies of both academics, it was Akhenaton, rather than Moses, who first introduced the notion of a monotheistic deity. Both scholars discussed the preexistence of the "42 Negative Confessions" (also known as the 42 Admonitions of Matt) predating Moses' formulation of the "Ten Commandments" atop Mount Sinai.

The seminary professor additionally highlighted that Constantine and the Pope devised a narrative, serving to establish the identity and divinity of Jesus. Arius, an African brother hailing from Libya, presented a counter-argument against the concept of Jesus' divinity. Arius observed that it was Constantine who expressed the desire to elevate the teachings of the Christian sect into the official religion of the state. This originated from adherents of Ptolemy I, who amalgamated the Greek Hellenistic faith with the enigmatic Egyptian religion, giving rise to the deity known as Serapis Christus. Ptolemy I constructed a monument within the sacred precincts of the temple in Memphis, Egypt. Arius, the African sibling, continually referenced Ausar as the source of Ptolemy's inspiration. The name Christian has its origins in the term Christus, and it refers to those who follow Serapis Christus.

Our esteemed professor imparted that the Egyptians declined to bestow the designation of Pharaoh upon Ptolemy I. Ptolemy I convened a council meeting, during which the bishops declined to perform the anointment. Subsequently, Ptolemy I orchestrated the demise of the bishops and subsequently arranged for another council meeting to take place, during which the attending bishops bestowed upon him the title of Pharaoh in 305 BCE. The professor stated that in the year 325 BCE, the Pope and Constantine collaborated to formulate the Nicaea Creed with the aim of resolving any potential contentions arising from Arius. The statement made by the professor was profoundly enlightening as it suggested that no tangible existence of Jesus was acknowledged or recorded until the Council of Nicaea.

The lecturer discussed Jesus in the context of fragmented writings that were gathered and assembled over an extended duration. He discerned instances of pseudepigraphy, namely the attribution of false authorial names to works within the Canon, including James, John I, and several others. It was brought to attention that the Pauline writings emerged half a century subsequent to the Common Era.

The Pauline writings, by virtue of advanced textual critique, were composed at distinct historical moments and are not attributable to a singular author. The epistles attributed to Paul preceded the composition of the Gospels. I acquired the information and placed it on the shelf for the purpose of safeguarding. I had the privilege of listening to a knowledgeable individual who expressed the belief that God's benevolence was manifest in the manifestation of the narrative propagated by the Pope and Constantine. This narrative, while not objectively true, held spiritual value as it served to safeguard the spiritual well-being of those who embraced it. I have frequently expressed the notion that there exists a modicum of veracity within falsehood. Furthermore, there is a certain degree of falsehood inherent even within the confines of veracity. The divine essence imbued the truth within the falsehood, granting it spiritual actuality, as the very fabric of the lie concealed profound spiritual verities.

I have participated in academic discourse through attending lectures delivered by Professor John H. Clarke, the esteemed historian, frequently underscored the fact that our ancestral predecessors, the African people, possessed a profound spiritual nature and intricately interwove spirituality into the fabric of their existence.

The ancient Greeks received their tutelage in the land of Egypt and assimilated the African principles of spirituality, subsequently fashioning their deities in accordance with their own cultural framework. Upon Constantine's proclamation of Christianity as the official faith, the narrative of Jesus emerged from an oral tradition originating in African folklore. The notion of Jesus' existence as a historical figure can be traced back to the formation of the Nicaea Council, where the consensus emerged to recognize him as a living human being. However, it is worth noting that this perspective challenges the idea of Jesus' pre-Nicaean existence as a factual reality.

Upon Arius's protestation, he cogently delineated the origins and circumstances surrounding the emergence of the diminutive Christian denomination. Professor Clarke held the view that the Nicene Creed was formulated in response to the arguments and objections put forth by Arius. The Vatican substituted the African Saints with sculptures and depictions of Europeans in order to exert control over the populace and amass riches.

The historical record establishes that Alexander the Great of Greece launched a military campaign into Egypt, resulting in the destruction of the libraries. Nevertheless, it has been unacknowledged by the general record that the Moors had purloined the knowledge of antiquity from the repositories of public history, subsequently restraining its dissemination and clandestinely disseminating it to India, Tibet, and various other regions of the globe, thus imparting enlightenment to the general populace. The establishment of the initial universities in Spain, as well as the instruction in various disciplines including mathematics, science, physics, geometry, anatomy, and astronomy, can be credited to the Moors. They ushered the Europeans out of a period of intellectual stagnation, enlightening them regarding matters of personal cleanliness.

The individual of African descent (referred to as a Moor) held dominion for a span of 700 years, fostering widespread education among the populace. The Moors were the ones who imparted the Europeans with the profound principles and teachings of the Masonic Order. Upon encountering visual depictions of the Moors donning turbans, European historians erroneously associated the Moors with Arab heritage. During the leadership of the Moors in Spain, diverse religious communities coexisted in a state of tranquility and amity. One of the lectures delivered by Dr. John Clarke highlighted the fact that the Moors had reached Spain five decades prior to the arrival of the Arabs. His assertions provide evidence to suggest that the Moors and Arabs were distinct entities.

Over time, as the Moors assumed positions of authority, a significant number amongst them succumbed to moral decay and indulged in corruption, ultimately divulging their secrets - exemplifying motifs akin to the story of Samson and Delilah. They were deprived of divine blessings. The groundwork had been laid for their deterioration.

As a result of the Pope's pursuit of power and influence, Spain was overthrown and the institution of the slave trade was established. The objective was to eliminate the conceptual frameworks acquired by the Moors through philosophical, religious, and spiritual teachings. The Pope established the Spanish Inquisitors, who subjected numerous individuals to public acts of brutal torture, massacres, and terror, surpassing the levels of cruelty seen under Hitler's regime. From that point forward, there have been, and currently exist, collective endeavors to systematically eliminate the historical records associated with the achievements in agriculture, mathematics, scientific inquiry, spiritual practices, medical knowledge, and technological advancements of the Kemetic civilization. If Europeans and European-Americans are unable to shift their perspective and acknowledge it as their own expression of creativity, they will continue to conceal and undermine the truth.

In his notable publication titled "Golden Age of the Moor," Ivan Van Sertima asserts that the possession of knowledge derived from Moorish medical literature was a prerequisite for medical degrees at Europe's esteemed universities throughout numerous centuries. Moreover, he contends that the legacy of Moorish domination in Spain faced erasure as a result of Catholic animosity, driven by Vatican-influenced politics and the aspiration for national unity.

Dr. Martin Luther King, Jr. expressed this sentiment in the following manner. One day, an untruth was uttered by someone. They expressed their thoughts using carefully chosen words. They rendered everything dark, unsightly, and malevolent. Please reference your dictionaries to explore the various synonyms associated with the term "black." It consistently denotes actions or traits that are disgraceful, abhorrent, and suggestive of malicious intent. Direct your attention to the term "white." The term "white" is commonly linked to purity, elevated status, and cleanliness. "I aim to utilize appropriate language tonight." It is disheartening that a portion of our population continues to hold onto this falsehood.

There is a current initiative aimed at continuously manipulating our beliefs in order to perpetuate falsehoods. William Cullen Bryant's statement, which I wholeheartedly concur with, posits that indeed, truth that has been suppressed will inevitably resurface. Furthermore, it is worth mentioning that Dr. Dinkins occasionally incorporated the words of Henry Wadsworth Longfellow into his sermons. The workings of the divine are characterized by a gradual but thorough progression. While divine intervention may unfold at a seemingly unhurried pace, it remains resolute, continuous, and dedicated to rectifying injustices.

We should proceed by posing the ensuing inquiries. What methods can we employ to access our spiritual reservoirs and attain comparable outcomes to those achieved by our predecessors, prior to their subversion by malevolent spiritual influences that hold sway over influential positions? In what ways can we engage in meditation and prayer to cultivate a prayerful existence and effective means of communication that guide us towards spiritual liberation, financial autonomy, and societal concordance? The quest for liberation from the relentless and cutthroat nature of our society, the pursuit of release from a manipulative construct that subjugates our minds, utilizing us as mere resources and means for profitable exploitation, widening the wealth gap and perpetuating an illusory sense of personal agency and liberty.

We are currently residing within a network of interconnected systems on a global scale. We exist within a complex societal construct that influences us through the dissemination of information via the media, the influence of the entertainment industry, the presence of chemicals in our food, the administration of vaccines, as well as the ubiquity of chemical emissions in the air we inhale and the water we consume.

The situation in Flint, Michigan has not occurred by chance. It was developed with the intention of serving as a protocol. The deliberate separation of over a thousand young children, including infants, from their immigrant parents at the southern border, subsequent confinement in containment facilities, and the possible involvement of some in illicit human trafficking activities cannot be attributed to mere happenstance. The announcement and dissemination of information concerning the coronavirus is not coincidental. Mass gatherings are being annulled, individuals are practicing self-isolation, and public sporting events are being suspended without any objections. These techniques correspond to a protocol aimed at manipulating the population through the utilization of fear. The coronavirus is real. People dying is real. I am of the opinion that this is a strategic move aimed at establishing the New World Order by introducing a solution and subsequently providing individuals with justification to undergo the implantation of microchips in their bodies. The concept is commonly referred to as the Hegelian dialectic of ordo-ab-chao, which elucidates the process through crisis-response-resolution.

From my perspective, supported by thorough examination and extensive scholarly inquiry, it is evident that society is progressively gravitating towards harnessing the potential of publicly acknowledged artificial intelligence to establish a law enforcement apparatus with the capacity to safeguard, shield, and execute with ruthless precision the objectives it has been specifically programmed to safeguard. The incidence of black individuals being fatally harmed by law enforcement officers is not a coincidental occurrence. We are individuals who embrace a deep sense of spirituality. We pose a significant spiritual concern, as acknowledged by Dr. Frances Cress Welsing in her notable work, The Isis Papers. Additionally, she highlights our existence as a genetic concern.

In the ensuing times, there shall exist automatons endowed with artificial intelligence that will engage in combat and uphold societal harmony, devoid of consciousness. There will be autonomous, robotic creatures designed to assail specific genetic demographics of individuals. We resemble amphibians in a heated container that is gradually approaching a boiling point.

Individuals who are recipients of public welfare benefits or government stipends (such as a pension, regular salary, or social security) will be mandated to undergo the insertion of a computer chip in order to receive their payments. The chip will be required for accessing and receiving healthcare services, exercising voting rights, enrolling in cost-free educational programs, and engaging in commercial transactions within marketplaces. In a manner similar to the transition from cash payments to the requisite establishment of bank accounts, and with the growing obsolescence of check-writing practices, it is foreseeable that physical currency in the form of paper money and coins will gradually fade away.

I contend that reality shows have instilled the notion within a significant portion of our population that it is socially acceptable to permit the presence of cameras in our private residences, whereby our personal activities are exposed to public scrutiny. We utilize social media platforms to promote our business and openly discuss our challenges. We install surveillance cameras within our residential premises. The concept of the "intelligent" residence incurs a cost.

As we progress through this era of technology, it becomes imperative that we dismantle and subsequently reconstruct our current communities, cities, and infrastructures as we prepare for the advent of a new era focused on space exploration and development. Climate change and the deliberate alteration of atmospheric conditions will serve as instrumental means to accomplish this transformation in a negative manner. People will die.

Please exercise caution regarding the United States and its participation in significant conflicts that have originated from the deliberate dissemination of falsehoods in order to elicit our engagement. General Colin Powell was likewise ensnared by a contrived falsehood, readily apparent to the public, with the apparent intention of obliterating any prospects of his ascension to the presidency of the United States.

Prayer and meditation serve as instrumental means by which individuals can achieve a profound connection with the divine. Prayer and meditation are integrated techniques that yield strength. This power operates with an imperceptible strength to rectify injustices, to rectify distorted circumstances, to alleviate difficulties, and to liberate us from the constraints of this materialistic realm of enslavement.

It is imperative for each of us to nurture our inner selves and recognize our role as essential participants in the revolutionary forces of God's Spiritual Army. The conflict at hand does not entail physical combat, as articulated by the Apostle Paul. We are engaged in a profound struggle that transcends physical adversaries. Our opponents are not mere mortal beings, but rather entities of authority, forces, and influential individuals who operate in the realms of obscurity and spiritual malevolence that permeate our world.

Dr. Dinkins previously expressed the viewpoint that malevolent forces can become personified within individuals. This sentiment aligns with the words of British historian John Dalberg-Acton, who asserted that the possession of power has a tendency to corrupt, and the possession of absolute power invariably corrupts without fail.

Power is not easily relinquished. There exists a longstanding verity that resonates as follows: "The missionaries bestowed upon us the Holy Bible, urging us to engage in devout contemplation through the act of prayer while shutting our eyes." Upon awakening, we found ourselves dispossessed of our territory, with only the Holy Bible remaining in our possession. However, the supplication I am referring to does not align with the aforementioned circumstances. I am referring to the act of maintaining possession of your Bible, entering into a private space, and engaging in a practice of deep reflection and communication with the Divine through meditation and prayer. Upon emerging from the confines of your private refuge, you shall not only reclaim the verities upheld within the sacred scriptures, but also retrieve the vast expanse of your territory, the essence of your being, your innate connection to the divine, and every other aspect of your existence that was wrongfully taken away. You shall remain impervious to the annihilation inflicted by the gates of inferno. Hence, the purpose of authoring this book becomes apparent.

The Lord's Prayer serves as a metaphorical covering. It harbors an inherent pathway leading to liberation. I acknowledge that not all individuals will perceive, comprehend, or adhere to it. Nonetheless, individuals who are currently embarking on their own personal journey, individuals who are contemplating embarking on such a journey, individuals who have abandoned their journey, individuals who have encountered setbacks along their journey, or individuals who are uncertain about the nature of their journey, may find solace in the fact that by reading this book, they may uncover valuable insights that will contribute to their personal growth and development.

Transcendental Meditation

Transcendental meditation, conceived by Maharishi Mahesh Yogi, constitutes a variant of mantra meditation.

The fundamental principle underlying this technique can be summarized as follows: allocate 40 minutes per day, dividing it equally into two 20-minute sessions, one in the morning and one in the evening—although it is permissible to engage in practice at any other suitable time. During these sessions, concentrate your awareness on a chosen word or phrase in a manner akin to the focused attention employed in breath mindfulness meditation.

Allow me to present the recommended approach to engaging in transcendental meditation:

How to

Engage in this meditation in the following manner:

Step 1

Please adhere to the prescribed protocols for meditation preparation which are consistent in most meditation practices, including: relocating to your designated meditation space, setting a timer, assuming a relaxed posture, attaining a state of calmness, and commencing by directing your concentration towards your breath. This particular aspect of meditation exhibits infrequent variations.

Step 2

Once you have achieved a greater sense of tranquility and alignment with your breath and the current state of being, redirect your attention towards your chosen mantra. A mantra can be described as a concise phrase or single word. In the traditional context of Transcendental Meditation, the mantra is a Sanskrit term imparted to a practitioner by an instructor.

One may opt for any phrase that holds significant personal significance, encompassing words such as peace, happiness, wellness, or mindfulness, among others. Alternatively, one may select from a diverse range of Sanskrit mantras available. Additionally, you have the option to employ a nonsensical term with the ultimate goal of providing your mind with a focal point to direct its current state of consciousness.

Step 3

Close your eyes and calmly begin to repeat or softly vocalize the mantra you have chosen, while being fully conscious of the sensory experience evoked by each individual letter within your chosen mantra. Harmonize your respiration and cognitive processes with this sacred incantation. For example, if your chosen affirmation is "stress free," during the inhalation, it is advisable to mentally picture inhaling serenity and tranquility while exhaling any symptoms of stress and anxiety during the exhalation.

Engage in this form of meditation, focusing solely on your chosen mantra for the entire duration of your meditation practice. To avoid repetition, allow the mind to freely wander without judgment, and kindly guide it back to the mantra, whether you are mentally or verbally repeating it.

By directing your focus onto a single word, you will experience a notable enhancement in your overall state of wellness, characterized by the profound alleviation of stress. This augmented sense of tranquility will heighten your overall sense of wellbeing and foster a stronger connection to the present moment, as well as a greater sense of purpose in your life.

Breathing & Meditation

Were you aware that one of the significant transformations in our lives occurred immediately upon our birth, as we commenced the act of respiration? Curiously, we were never instructed in the art of respiration.

Regrettably, the significance and purpose of breathing in our lives often go unrecognized. The act of respiration serves as a fundamental pillar of our existence, as it is through this process that we obtain a vital infusion of oxygen within our beings, the absence of which would render our survival utterly impossible. In the practice of meditation, the act of breathing assumes significant importance, serving as a foundational element that holds tremendous influence over our existence. By delving into the intricacies of our breath, mastering the art of directing our attention towards it, and comprehending its profound repercussion on our lives, we have the potential to enact transformative changes within ourselves.

Breathing techniques are incorporated in various forms of meditation, encompassing breath meditation as well. The practice of breath meditation is a distinctive form of meditation that is widely accessible and embraced across the globe. One distinguishing characteristic of breath meditation lies in its divergence from the utilization of specific objects, mantras, or visualization techniques by the meditator. In this particular scenario, the individual engaged in meditation typically directs their awareness towards their breathing, devoting their complete attention to this involuntary bodily activity.

The efficacy of incorporating breathing into meditation lies in the physiological movements it induces, the provision of air to the body, and the meditator's capacity to concentrate solely on the act of breathing, thereby diverting attention from any other mental activities and sources of disruption. Furthermore, through the act of respiration, individuals can gain insight into the correlation between their breath and their emotional state. Consequently, you can acquire the capacity to develop novel respiratory methods through the efficient utilization of the lungs.

Are you familiar with the notion that individuals often engage in deep inhalation and exhalation when experiencing stress or engaging in physical activity? If an inquiry is made, they will assertively express that they have indeed encountered alterations throughout these sessions. While numerous individuals engage in this practice either as a technique or an exercise, it bears resemblance to meditation; the only distinction lies in their lack of awareness.

When engaging in the act of meditation, optimal outcomes are achieved by directing one's attention towards the process and rhythmic pattern of inhalation and exhalation, maintaining conscious awareness of this process, assuming a proper seated posture, and gently closing the eyes.

As previously stated, the subsequent section expounds on the application of breathing in the context of meditation:

• Directing one's attention to the act of breathing, maintaining a single-minded focus on this particular aspect of consciousness.

• Directing focus towards the respiratory patterns and the subsequent bodily reactions. For instance, the movements of diagrams, the respiration process of the lungs, and occasionally the movements of the eyes.

• Engaging in controlled respiration while concurrently directing one's attention towards an alternative entity, concept, or location.

- Making use of the respiratory system and formulating innovative methods of inhaling and exhaling.

- Trying to experience how you body, emotions or feelings change

- Endeavoring to elicit emotions through the utilization of a particular breathing technique.

During the practice of meditation, it is recommended to engage in natural breathing, which is most ideally achieved by inhaling and exhaling through the nostrils. One should refrain from attempting to manipulate the respiratory process, but instead focus on developing an awareness of the flow of air in and out of the body, which becomes the focal point of the meditation practice.

If one were to consider the correlation between respiration and our physical being, it becomes evident that the level of breath intensity tends to increase during instances of anger, concern, tension, anxiety, and distress. However, in a state of tranquility, composure, and freedom, respiration assumes a subtle character, where physical motions are barely discernible. Furthermore, during the periods of running or engaging in physical labor, the respiratory rate and depth of breath increase. These circumstances exemplify the interconnectedness of respiration with the entirety of the human body. An atmosphere of tension, restlessness, anxiety, and concern, among others. Corresponds to our emotional state; given that our emotional well-being impacts our respiration, it suggests a profound interdependence between breathing and emotions.

Guidelines for proper respiration during the practice of meditation

Herein are recommendations on incorporating breathing techniques into the practice of meditation:

• Breathe in a quiet and deliberate manner, ensuring that the inhalation is executed slowly and with precision. Such controlled breathing should be practiced to the extent that even a thread positioned directly in front of the nose would remain undisturbed.

• It is important to consistently observe a brief pause after each round of inhalation and exhalation, by consciously holding your breath for a few seconds.

• While inhaling, endeavor to experience a sense of introducing novel and invigorating elements into your existence, specifically, boundless tranquility.

• During exhalation, visualize and experience the act of releasing any emotional tension, agitation, or sensations that you deem necessary to relinquish.

• During the subsequent phase of inhalation, envision the infusion of cosmic energy within you, and as you exhale, perceive the departure of pain, fear, desolation, and anguish.

• Sustain a steady rhythm of inhalation and exhalation, while perceiving a glorious infusion of celestial vitality, boundless elation, optimal well-being, and profound contentment with each repetition. For optimal sensation, envision the assimilation of the stimulus permeating every crevice of your being, imbuing gratification and fostering improvement. Likewise, during exhalation, envision a cleansing process wherein you expunge any lingering feelings of guilt, all impure deeds, actions incompatible with divinity, and any undesirable elements residing within your physical being.

Ultimately, it is crucial to bear in mind that one will encounter hindrances upon embarking on the journey of meditation. For instance, you might encounter difficulty in directing your attention towards the process of breathing or maintaining concentration on a single thought. Nevertheless, through diligent effort, you will acquire the capability to evaluate and ascertain whether you are making any advancements. As your proficiency improves, you will gradually transcend the physical constraints that bind the majority of us, unbeknownst to our consciousness. One of the remarkable aspects of practicing breathing meditation lies in its accessibility and affordability.

Mitigating Discomfort And Minimizing Distractions Exercise

Whilst engaged in the practice of meditation, it is possible to experience sensations and thoughts that may elicit discomfort or unease. Exercise caution in acknowledging the restlessness of your mind, and its ability to compel your body to engage in specific movements and experiences. In the event that you encounter intrusive thoughts or visualizations, it is advisable to refrain from developing any attachment to them, as such phenomena are transient and will inevitably diminish in due course. If their persistence continues, it is advisable to maintain an objective and detached stance while observing their actions. Furthermore, one may contemplate, "Whom does the current experience belong to?"

Please refrain from ruminating on a distressing incident. As you continue to deliberate upon it, your agitation intensifies, consequently amplifying the event's impact. Direct your attention back to the task at hand, and its impact will diminish.

In the event that you possess any apprehensions, you may choose to document them for future reference and address them subsequently. Furthermore, it is possible to remind oneself, "I shall address matters as they arise," as an alternative approach. In instances where excessive anticipation is placed upon the act of meditation, reiterating the phrase, "I hold no preconceived notions or assumptions," can prove to be effective. The consistent utilization of such affirmations can greatly facilitate the liberation of one's mind.

You may also envision your intrusive thoughts, recollections, emotions, and sensations as undesired plants amidst a cultivated garden. When something captures your attention, assign it a categorization (such as: exasperating reminiscence, novel concept, fanciful notion) and subsequently eliminate it. Devote yourself to nurturing the cognitive sanctuary within your consciousness by discerning and eliminating sources of diversion.

Labeling

One approach to maintaining awareness of things without being emotionally impacted by them is by assigning labels to them. This does not imply categorizing them as positive, negative, enjoyable, or unenjoyable, but rather designating them impartially. Once an individual assigns a measure of significance to certain entities or experiences, their emotional responses will become active and potentially alter their interpretation.

When something causes you distress, assign it a proper designation. Additionally, you have the ability to modify your convictions concerning the matter in order to achieve the intended outcomes. Express it as follows: "Allow me to articulate the matter at hand by stating, 'This pertains to my (specify issue here)." "It is likely that the situation will naturally resolve itself, as it frequently does. Therefore, I must persist and continue forward." Speaking to oneself in such a manner can enhance one's mental discipline and influence over one's thoughts.

Types Of Meditation

A comprehensive range of meditation techniques should be taken into account. Certain individuals may necessitate the maintenance of a motionless bodily state, or the engagement of thought processes within confined parameters, whereas other variants afford unrestricted bodily movement. Despite sharing a common objective of enhancing inner peace, these approaches exhibit notable variations. It is essential that you make an effort to explore various styles and techniques in order to determine which ones are most suitable for you.

There exists a viewpoint among certain individuals that equates meditation to sustenance. There exist particular types that demonstrate superior performance when contrasted with others, whereas certain kinds yield consistent outcomes among all individuals. Essentially, the primary aim of meditation is to cultivate mental clarity and liberate oneself from the burdens of stress and anxiety resulting from routine engagements.

Commence locating a serene and cozy location. Certain individuals may prefer to recline during their meditation practice. In the event that you perceive yourself experiencing drowsiness while reclining, it is advisable to assume an upright position. Select a meditation technique that is most suited to your needs and preferences.

Mindfulness Meditation

This particular form of meditation arises from the lineage of the Buddhist tradition. It is widely recognized as the most prevalent form of meditation. One acquires the ability to embrace the present moment while being cognizant of surrounding circumstances, disregarding their significance. This particular form of thinking can be considered as a state of flow, whereby the mind is allowed to transition seamlessly from one thought to another, without fixating on any particular object or topic.

If one presently resides in close proximity to a bustling thoroughfare, there is no necessity to endeavor in preventing the intrusion of external noises originating from vehicles, or the boisterous exclamations of individuals into one's consciousness. Allow your consciousness to become cognizant of those elements. Direct your attention towards your emotions or personal encounters. Expand your consciousness by acknowledging and embracing the thoughts that arise within your mind, allowing them to naturally dissipate.

Through the practice of mindfulness meditation, one undergoes a process of training oneself to cultivate mindfulness and consciously direct one's attention to the present moment in all activities. This fosters an enhanced mindfulness of one's surroundings and a heightened sense of calmness in the body. This meditation facilitates the development of mental and physical faculties to engage in contemplation over aspects of your life that lie beyond your power to alter, even including those within your sphere of total influence.

Mantra Meditation

Mantras are comprised of verbal utterances, expressions, or notions that an individual consistently recites in a silent or audible manner during the practice of meditation. While the act of producing sounds during the practice of meditation may appear unconventional, it should be understood that these auditory stimuli effectively function as focal points, facilitating the expulsion of disruptive negative thoughts. The mantra 'Om' is frequently utilized in the practice of yoga owing to its profound vibrational properties, which facilitate enhanced concentration on its sonority.

Transcendental meditation is a specific form of mantra meditation. Assuming an upright posture and articulating invocations with proper alignment contributes to the attainment of mental clarity and heightened consciousness.

Guided Meditation

This form of meditation is alternatively recognized as guided visualization or guided imagery. It entails directing attention towards a specific visual or mental representation, which elicits a sense of solace, by engaging the senses. This process can be accomplished through actively engaging with a meditation instructor or guide, or by utilizing an audio recording, while simultaneously employing a visualization technique wherein one envisions oneself traversing a vast expanse resembling an open field, with graceful avian creatures soaring majestically overhead, against the backdrop of a serene cerulean firmament. One can alternatively focus on their breath without necessitating its utilization or regulation, as the sensations experienced are purely fictitious in nature. It originates solely from your mind.

Zen Meditation

Zen meditation is a globally observed practice that involves assuming a seated posture, cultivating a receptive state of mind and body, and nurturing a profound exploration of one's holistic existence. You assume various postures as prescribed, while making a concerted effort to detach your mind from any stray thoughts or mental imagery. After a brief interval, it will become evident that your cardiac rhythm decelerates, and your respiration transitions to a shallower pattern, eventually leading you to attain a state of meditation. You develop an heightened awareness of the present moment and respond accordingly to the prevailing circumstances. You are freed from any concerns regarding past events and future outcomes. This method typically serves as an effective means of distancing oneself from the cacophony emanating from the recesses of the subconscious.

Tai Chi

Tai Chi is a gentle variation of Chinese martial arts. One engages in a deliberate and elegant execution of a sequence of motions or poses, accompanied by deliberate and controlled respiration.

Qi Gong

This particular meditation technique aligns with that of Taoist meditation practices, as well as being intrinsic to the realm of traditional Chinese medicine. It encompasses the integration of mindfulness practice, controlled respiration techniques, progressive muscle relaxation, and kinesthetic activities. The objective of this endeavor is to regain and perpetuate equilibrium. Through the act of respiration, the vital force is dispersed within the bodily organs and centers, influencing both the corporeal and ethereal aspects of your being. Nevertheless, it is unrelated to emotions. Additionally, direct your focus towards the midpoint of your forehead, the region encompassing your chest, as well as the area situated below your navel.

Yoga

The act of transitioning between various postures while maintaining control over one's breath necessitates both focus and equilibrium. Yoga enhances bodily flexibility while promoting a centered and tranquil state of mind, focused on the present.

By Means Of The Virtue Of Forgiveness, Tranquility

Your capacity for granting forgiveness may prove to be the most valuable gift you can bestow upon yourself during this festive period. It facilitates the release of detrimental emotions and thoughts, encompassing anger, resentment, bitterness, shame, grief, regret, and guilt.

If one perceives that they have been unjustly treated by another individual, they might believe that overcoming this grievance is an insurmountable task. It is possible that you would persist in pondering over the betrayal, even after the initial anger it provoked has diminished, instead of allowing it to gradually recede from your recollection.

Conversely, the act of extending forgiveness to others can serve as a potent mechanism that enhances your holistic state of being. In the act of forgiving someone, you are deliberately choosing to relinquish any adverse sentiments you may have harbored towards them, irrespective of the justification for such emotions.

Your inherent ability to grant forgiveness instills belief that forgiveness is indeed achievable, notwithstanding the arduous nature of the endeavor. There is a correlation between forgiveness and enhancements in both physical and mental well-being. It truly astonishes how certain individuals possess the ability to either overlook or pardon certain things. Pardoning is a therapeutic antidote that can be administered to the physical, cognitive, and metaphysical aspects.

What is the underlying rationale for embracing forgiveness? An increasing body of evidence suggests that the long-term retention of traumatic memories and feelings of resentment can have deleterious impacts on an individual's overall well-being.

"When we extend forgiveness to others, it yields several advantageous outcomes for our psychological well-being, as outlined below:

Lessens stress level
Retaining feelings of anger and resentment not only undermines interpersonal relationships, but also exerts physiological strain on the individual, with potential correlations to the development of malignant conditions and various ailments. By relinquishing your anger and resentment, you can alleviate stress by relinquishing the influence that the other individual or circumstance holds over you.

Enhances proficiency in managing anger Enhances skills in anger management Promotes the development of anger management abilities Cultivates effective anger management skills Fosters the acquisition of anger management competencies

Your ability to release negative emotions and progress in your life will lead to elevated levels of contentment. Based on a multitude of research studies, individuals who possess an inclination towards animosity and resentment are prone to encountering physical afflictions.

Diminishes the indicators and manifestations of depression and anxiety.

The act of forgiveness bestows upon us the gifts of healing and grace, while replacing depression with a renewed sense of purpose and compassion. An additional prevalent source of anxiety stems from the apprehension that we have mishandled a certain facet of the circumstance. Our culpable conscience instigates profound unease. The capacity to grant forgiveness to others facilitates a heightened sense of self-love, thereby alleviating the internal anguish we bear.

Mitigates the impact of persistent pain.

Based on clinical observations, it has been noted that a considerable proportion of patients experiencing chronic pain encounter challenges in forgiving individuals whom they perceive to have caused them harm or injustice. Based on these research findings, it can be reliably assessed that the act of pardoning others remains achievable in individuals enduring persistent pain.

Refines well-being

The process of attaining emotional forgiveness entails substituting negative sentiments of unforgiveness with more constructive emotions centered around others. Pardoning at an emotional level entails alterations to an individual's psychophysiology, yielding more immediate repercussions on an individual's health and overall welfare. By relinquishing our resentments, we contribute to fostering a greater level of harmony in all aspects of the world. Nightmares dissipate, giving way to exhilarating prospects for one's future. After participating in this retreat, we find ourselves in a state of increased comfort, contentment, and a greater willingness to extend philanthropy and affection towards the world.

Indeed, the act of pardoning another individual can be accomplished by merely consciously choosing to release any resentment, anguish, or inclination for retaliation. It holds significance to the process of healing as it allows for the release of adverse emotions, facilitating the progression towards embracing a new chapter in life. These emotions may encompass anger, guilt, shame, sadness, or any other prevailing sentiment that one may be undergoing.

Anxiety Alleviation through Guided Affirmation Meditation

Assume a comfortable posture, ideally seated on a chair with your legs crossed.

- Inhale gradually and profoundly. When experiencing anxiety, your respiration will accelerate and become rapid. By engaging in slow and deep respiration, you gradually alleviate feelings of anxiety and panic.

- Following a deliberate and measured inhalation. Engage in a brief moment of introspection, contemplating your thoughts, experiences, and the events that transpired throughout the day.

- As you engage in this activity, a plethora of thoughts, concerns, and inquiries inundate your mind.
- Instruct your mind to desist. - Command your mind to cease. - Direct your mind to halt. - Order your mind to refrain. - Advise your mind to terminate its activity. Please articulate your words in a manner that reflects authority and assertiveness.
- While issuing this directive, you experience the liberation of your mind from these thoughts and concerns. - As you issue this command, you sense your mind beginning to release these thoughts and worries. - During the act of issuing this command, you perceive the commencement of your mind's release from these thoughts and worries. - As you dictate this command, you become aware of your mind initiating the process of releasing these thoughts and worries. - When you issue this command, you can sense your mind starting to let go of these thoughts and worries. You commence to experience

the perception arising from a void mental state.

- As you commence your cognitive blankness, proceed by methodically arranging your thoughts - As you engage in the process of organizing each thought, express a word of positive affirmation for every individual thought.

- As an example, one might initiate the process of organizing their thoughts by prioritizing the payment of bills.

- As you gather and structure your ideas, commence the process of reaffirmation.

I have full control over my financial matters." "I possess full autonomy in managing my financial resources." "I exercise complete authority over my monetary affairs." "I am firmly in command of my financial situation." "I have absolute mastery over my finances."

- With each iteration of reciting your affirmations, be sure to contemplate their meaning. Please shut your eyes and envision the sensation of being in command of one's financial matters.

- At this juncture, release any pessimistic notions from your consciousness. Given that you continue to keep your eyes shut, I urge you to reflect upon those past instances when you exhibited adeptness in managing your financial affairs. I kindly request you to envision the most recent occasion on which you promptly settled your financial obligations, and reflect upon the emotions you experienced during that period.

- Presently, you have regained a sense of wellness, and your previous concerns regarding your invoice have been alleviated. You redirect your focus towards your mind and proceed to organize your thoughts further.

- It could be that your subsequent consideration pertains to your relationship, inducing anxiety regarding its potential culmination.

- Maintain a positive outlook regarding your relationship, focusing on the positives and cherishing the shared experiences and memories with your partner.

- While engaging in this introspection, it serves as a gentle yet poignant reminder that you possess an exquisite essence and an enchanting smile.

- Commence your affirmations by recalling those elements you can readily recollect. - Initiate your affirmations by starting with the recollection of those aspects within your memory. - You kick-start your affirmations by commencing them with the remembrance of those particulars.

I possess an exquisite essence and a charming countenance."

I possess a strong sense of self-worth and I readily relinquish any feelings of inadequacy stemming from my past mistakes."

I express my heartfelt appreciation towards my partner, and I am filled with utmost gratitude for the profound love that binds us."

I hold the same affection for my partner as I do for myself."

- At this juncture, it is imperative that you possess a comprehensive comprehension of every statement you utter and permit it to reverberate within you. One starts to envision the initial encounter with their significant other, contemplating the act of bestowing a warm smile upon them. It is also imperative to remember that prioritizing self-love is essential prior to extending love to others.

- At present, you have successfully alleviated the strain and apprehension within your relationship. You exhibit a considerable improvement compared to your initial state - You direct your attention towards your mental faculties and steadfastly arrange your ideas.

- It is evident that you recall engaging in a contentious exchange with your superior earlier today, which has left you feeling infuriated. - In order to alleviate this emotion, I suggest the deliberate and gradual inhalation followed by a relieved exhalation. This process induces a sense of relaxation, allowing the release of anger. - As you continue, please commence the practice of positive affirmations by declaring, "I possess a rational and well-functioning intellect, and I am deserving of affection and regard."

I relinquished all internal stress, indignation, and apprehension."

I possess a formidable intellect and am on par with any individual, holding no sense of inferiority."

I possess wisdom and possess the competence to efficiently resolve problems."

I possess formidable fortitude, akin to that of the mighty eagle."

I solely entertain affirmative words and thoughts within my mind.

I remain unaffected by the adverse thoughts and words expressed by individuals in my vicinity."

- While reciting these affirmations, it is advised to inhale deeply following the articulation of each statement. Following a calming inhalation, envision the experience of possessing a sound state of mind and being worthy of affection.

Envision a scenario where you approach your supervisor the following day, and all instances of disagreement are promptly resolved.

Contemplate being recognized as the most exceptional employee by year-end.

- As you contemplate these scenarios, you will witness a gradual alleviation of your fears and challenges, descending upon the terrestrial realm. You are starting to experience a sense of joy at this moment.

- You redirect your attention towards your thoughts in order to arrange the subsequent idea. You appear to be harboring concerns regarding your forthcoming journey. You are unfamiliar with the progress of the excursion or its potential outcomes - Commence your affirmations with expressions of gratitude towards nature, the sun, the moon, and the stars.

I am greatly pleased to embark on this journey, and I hold firm conviction that it shall prove to be a profoundly beautiful experience."

I grant permission to my body and mind to indulge in this journey."

I exercise patience in allowing my body to acclimate to the journey for optimal comfort."

I possess inherent sociability, which facilitates my ability to establish friendships with unfamiliar individuals."

I possess an inherent quality that elicits affection, thereby prompting strangers to harbor fondness towards me."

- As you commence, please bear in mind to inhale deeply and exhale audibly while reciting these affirmations. As you engage in this practice, begin the process of analyzing and envisioning each affirmation. Envision yourself in a scenario where you are seated on an airplane, and your fellow passenger shares the same passions and interests as you do. He/she holds identical values as yourself - - Envision your host exhibiting a wide smile and expansive embrace. As you arrive at your destination, your host welcomes you with a big hug, wraps your shoulders in her arms.

- Envisioning these concepts, a sense of ease is engendered and mental distress is alleviated. - Inhale deeply and exhale deliberately. - Direct your attention inward, fixate upon your cognitive faculties, and assess the presence of any unorganized thoughts lingering within your consciousness.

- In the absence of any of these, inhale deeply and exhale while extending a broad smile. - In the presence of any of these, it is advisable to persist in proclaiming affirmations corresponding to each of your thoughts. - Direct your attention towards your musculature and physical being. Throughout the entirety of the day, you have exhibited signs of unease, resulting in the tightening of your muscles.

- Direct your attention towards your toes and experience the sensation of tension in that area. Inhale deeply and exhale, experiencing a sense of release - Commence your affirmations by articulating "I grant permission for my body to experience comfort."

My body alleviates any tension, fatigue, and discomfort.

I derive great pleasure from experiencing a tranquil and supple physique, and with each exhalation, I sense the dissipation of all bodily tensions."

I am neither fatigued nor experiencing anxiety."

As you engage in the recitation of these affirmations, you may begin by invoking positive statements regarding the various regions of your physique. For instance, you may affirm "My shoulder possesses a generous width, and I am consciously releasing any underlying tension within it."

My toes are diminutive and minuscule, and I grant them the luxury of reaching a state of relaxation."

I possess a stable state of mind and I do not experience any feelings of anxiety.

I alleviate the strain in my lower limbs."

In the present moment, while I am upright and moving, I am experiencing a sense of ease and contentment."

- While reciting these affirmations, you experience the gradual release of all tension residing within your body.

- Inhale deeply and exhale slowly - By doing so, you have effectively released all anxieties that were occupying your mental and physical state.

Positive declarations for expeditious relaxation during work hours

It is possible to engage in meditation during one's work hours as well. Engaging in workplace meditation brings about an alleviation of stress.

Steps

- Take a seat in your chair and ensure you are properly situated and at ease. - Direct your attention inward by shutting your eyes and inhaling deeply and steadily. - Concentrate on each breath, savoring the audible release accompanying every exhalation. Experience the tactile perception accompanying inhalation and exhalation - Permit your thoughts to find tranquility and embrace a sense of ease - Commence your affirmations by uttering "I possess ambition and prioritize my professional advancement"

I am actively striving to actualize my aspirations." "I am diligently exerting myself towards the realization of my ambitions." "I am earnestly working towards achieving the fulfillment of my personal goals." "I am resolutely pursuing the manifestation of my aspirations.

I hold a deep appreciation for my occupation and derive great fulfillment from pursuing my passion."

I am confident in the exceptional abilities of my team, and together we are poised to accomplish remarkable objectives."

I am enthusiastic and optimistic about my work."

I derive motivation from my dreams" "I find inspiration in my dreams to drive me forward" "I am motivated by the pursuit of my dreams" "My dreams serve as a source of motivation for me"

I derive pleasure from engaging in work endeavors, and experience a sense of relaxation subsequent to each professional endeavor."

- While iterating these affirmations, allow them to deeply resonate within you.

- One can envision the sensation of achieving the pinnacle of their career, attaining the status of being an exemplary employee, and preparing themselves for the realization of their ambitious goals - One experiences immense satisfaction and a deep sense of happiness.

- Inhale deeply, releasing a sigh of relief as you exhale. - You proceed with these positive affirmations for the subsequent two minutes. - Once you have concluded the affirmations, take a deep inhalation and exhalation. - At this point, you are prepared to resume your tasks, experiencing a restored sense of energy and resilience. You have successfully alleviated your stress

Considering The Options Available For Fulfilling The Requirement

During this particular stage of motivation, the individual endeavors to examine various alternatives that have the potential to culminate in the desired outcome - that is, the fulfillment of the predetermined need. Indeed, it is the very necessity that guides individuals towards a desired course of action.

Choosing the goal
The third phase in the motivation process involves reaching a determination regarding the objective to strive for. In this case, the objectives are determined in accordance with the requirements, and subsequently, the action plan is carefully chosen.

Performance
During this fourth stage, the requirement, the strategy, and the intended outcome serve as the catalysts for achieving outstanding performance. All the actions undertaken in this stage are directed towards fulfilling the unaddressed requirement.

Consequences

The outcome of pursuing a particular course of action manifests itself as either retribution or accolade. Incentives are intended to motivate an individual to replicate their actions on subsequent occasions, while penalties are intended to dissuade a recurrence of the same behavior in the future.

Reevaluation of the necessity

Upon the conclusion of the need fulfillment process, it is imperative to assess whether the solution provided has effectively met the identified need during the initial phase. If a need remains unfulfilled, the process is reiterated.

Theories of Motivation

Motivational theories elucidate the factors that contribute to the appeal of one thing over another for an individual. Understanding the intricate factors contributing to motivation is imperative in comprehending the correlation between engaging in tasks that inspire you and achieving outstanding outcomes, as opposed to undertaking endeavors that fail to elicit motivation, which inevitably leads to subpar performance. Listed below are the various theories pertaining to motivation.

Maslow's Theory of Human Motivation

Abraham Maslow expounded upon this theory by categorizing all human needs into a hierarchical structure consisting of five distinct levels. According to this classification, individuals first address the needs located at the lower end, and subsequently progress towards those situated at the higher end, analogous to ascending a pyramid.

The lowest tier comprises physiological necessities, namely water, shelter, and sustenance. The second classification pertains to the requirements for security and safety, encompassing safeguards against theft and deprivation. The third classification comprises social necessities. These pertain to the requirements associated with love, activity, inclusion, and social connections. The fourth classification pertains to the requirement of self-esteem. In this context, an individual aspires for autonomy, liberty, accomplishment, standing, self-worth, and acknowledgement. The final classification is referred to as self-actualization. It represents a pivotal period wherein individuals come to recognize their utmost capabilities and aspire to assume a position of authority over others. An individual who has achieved self-actualization desires to possess control or influence.

In accordance with this theory, it is imperative to progress through the pyramid by satisfying the foundational needs prior to addressing those positioned at higher levels. Furthermore, once a need has been fulfilled, it ceases to act as a motivating force, thereby requiring individuals to seek motivation from needs that are situated at higher levels within the pyramid.

The Expectancy Theory

This theory postulates that an individual's inclination to dedicate effort towards fulfilling certain needs is contingent upon the factors of valence, expectancy, and instrumentality.

Motivation is determined by three factors, denoted symbolically as follows:

Motivation= $E*I*V$

where 'E' represents the anticipation that the outcome is a direct result of his exerted efforts

The relationship between the performance and acquiring the reward can be understood through the concept of 'I'.

'V' represents the monetary worth of the reward obtained

The Doctrine of Reinforcement

The theory in question was formulated by Thorndike, a renowned psychologist, in the year 1911. According to this postulation, conduct that is recognized and rewarded tends to be continuously exhibited. This theory encompasses the responses attributed to behavior as reinforcements, which can either be of a positive or negative nature.

Positive reinforcement is a highly regarded outcome intended to foster desirable conduct and enhance the likelihood of its recurrence. This can be achieved by expressing compliments, increasing salary, conducting a favorable performance evaluation, and providing letters of recommendation. Positive reinforcement should be earned. If not, it will hold no significance. As a result, in order to guarantee that the positive reinforcements yield the intended motivation, it is essential to ensure that the task itself is both stimulating and demanding.

Negative reinforcements are implemented through the practice of either withholding or withdrawing privileges. A few instances of adverse reinforcement encompass the act of dispatching intimidating communications as a means to compel an individual to fulfill their obligations, or terminating an individual's probationary status upon a noticeable enhancement in their performance.

Per the proposed theory, punishment is identified as an adverse outcome, which may be administered through assigning individuals tasks they find disagreeable, vocally reprimanding them, or withholding promised remuneration or promised items such as toys.

When administering negative reinforcement, it is possible to employ threats, which serve as a means of delivering punishment.

The theory of existential relatedness.

Alderfer formulated this theory whereby he posited that the three fundamental requirements of an individual are interconnectedness, subsistence, and evolution. The existence needs bear resemblance to the physiological needs in Maslow's hierarchy. Interacting with others fulfills the requirement for social connectedness. Some of these factors encompass self-esteem and prestige, among various others. Growth necessities refer to those which fulfill the needs for self-esteem and self-actualization.

The Impact of Motivation on Behavior

Various factors influence the resultant performance outcomes, such as the diverse attributes of motivation. The performance undergoes a transition, either progressing from poorer to enhanced behavioral persistence or experiencing a regression from improved to diminished performance. The attainment of a more favorable outcome results in an individual's contentment and heightened welfare. Therefore, it is imperative to duly consider the underlying intention behind an action and accurately ascertain the precise factors that will serve as motivation for an individual.

If you present them with a challenge that fails to elicit motivation, the resultant outcome is expected to be more unfavorable. Nevertheless, should you provide a compelling incentive, the individual will become enthused and produce a positive result.

Researchers have determined that individuals who initiate efforts towards external objectives, such as weight loss, commonly experience discontentment with the outcomes, irrespective of their level of adherence, self-esteem, or physical dimensions. One of the prevalent motivations individuals adopt exercise is the aspiration to shed pounds in order to enhance their physical appearance. Nevertheless, this strategy is not suitable. It is imperative that individuals' motivation be characterized by greater self-determination. This holds especially true for individuals who are not fully dedicated to exercising and engage in physical activity solely for the purpose of demonstrating to themselves and others that they are endeavoring to shed weight.

The situation varies when it pertains to individuals engaging in physical activity for the purpose of internal regulation. They incur higher levels of satisfaction and experience enhanced well-being.

It is an undeniable reality that a significant number of individuals may never develop a liking for physical exercise; nonetheless, they have the potential to cultivate an appreciation for it. When one develops an acknowledgment for physical activity, they commence perceiving themselves as an individual who engages in exercise, thereby shifting their perspective away from regarding it solely as a tool for attaining pre-established objectives. Engaging in such activities will provide you with the requisite contentment and drive necessary to maintain your efforts. Ultimately, you will also begin to experience weight reduction.

Hence, it is internal objectives rather than external ones that serve as the more efficient catalysts for motivation.

Powerful Meditation Tips

In the following chapter, you will acquire diverse techniques for engaging in the practice of meditation. Regardless of your location or the time, these suggestions can be utilized to assist you.

20 Tips for Hushing Your Mind

Meditation is commonly regarded as the practice of directing one's complete attention towards a singular point. The exercise regimen yields significant health advantages, encompassing enhanced focus, elevated mood, and reduced anxiousness. While it is true that a considerable number of individuals engage in meditation at some juncture in their lives, only a negligible proportion of these individuals persist with it for a sufficient duration to experience its advantages. This is highly regrettable, and it may potentially account for the apprehension individuals hold towards attempting it. Your mentality significantly impacts the outcome.

1. Please formalize the practice. To progress to the succeeding stage through meditation, it is imperative to allocate dedicated periods of time. I strongly recommend engaging in a practice session at least twice daily.

2. Initiate your practice by focusing on your breath. Deep and slow breathing

induces a state of muscular relaxation, thereby enhancing mental concentration and reducing heart rate. It serves as an excellent method to initiate your practice.

3. Ensure that you engage in a warm-up routine prior to commencing the activity. Engaging in stretching exercises effectively promotes muscle and tendon relaxation. It will facilitate a higher degree of comfort for sitting or reclining. Furthermore, direct your focus towards your physical well-being in conjunction with engaging in stretching exercises.

4. It is imperative to ensure that you engage in purposeful meditation. Novices should comprehend that meditation constitutes a form of proactive endeavor. The acquisition of

this skill requires considerable effort initially, necessitating deliberate and focused involvement.

5. Feelings of frustration may gradually arise. This phenomenon is frequently observed among novices. You might find yourself questioning the rationale behind your actions or why it proves to be significantly challenging for you to maintain focus. This serves as a mental exercise and will improve with repeated practice. Just focus harder.

6. Experience bodily sensations. It is highly beneficial for novices to attentively observe their physical state as the meditative state begins to establish its presence. Following the attainment of mental serenity, shift your focus towards your feet and proceed

gradually upwards along your physical form. Please ensure that the internal organs are included. This demonstrates a positive state of well-being and signifies that you, as a novice, are progressing in the right direction.

7. Engage in systematic exploration of different postures. The prevailing belief among the majority is that meditation entails assuming a Yoga posture with crossed legs, yet this perception is incorrect. One can engage in meditation while reclining, assuming a seated position on a chair, or adopting any other posture that provides optimal comfort.

8. Please select a specific room in which to conduct your meditation practice. It is imperative to ensure that the designated

room is strictly distinct from areas of work, sleep, or exercise. Kindly place your candles or additional spiritual artifacts within this designated area to foster a sense of tranquility.

9. Please acquaint yourself with the practice of meditation. Active participation will enhance your ability to concentrate and further deepen your understanding of this discipline.

10. Please demonstrate your dedication. The practice of meditation is a fundamental aspect of one's lifestyle, and one would not reap its rewards should they discontinue their engagement with it. It takes practice.

11. Please engage in the act of listening to serene music. Engaging in the act of attentively listening to instrumental music, characterized by its calming and tranquil nature, without any lyrical content, can enhance one's ability to concentrate. It facilitates the progression of your process.

12. Create instances of mindfulness throughout your day. Developing a habit of meditation can be significantly enhanced by practicing mindfulness or centering oneself in the present moment outside of dedicated meditation sessions.

13. Make sure there are no distractions. A prevalent error made by numerous novices is their failure to establish tranquility. Should you discover that you

have neglected to power off your mobile device or request a quiet environment, you will fail to achieve the necessary state of tranquility essential for your meditation practice to yield any substantial results.

14. Please take note of minor modifications. For those who are new to the practice, even the smallest adjustments have the potential to shift your meditation experience from one of frustration to a state of rejuvenation. These subtle modifications may appear inconspicuous to an external observer, yet they possess the potential to significantly impact the practitioner's meditative experience.

15. Utilize candles. Engaging in the practice of meditation with closed eyes

may present a certain level of difficulty to individuals who are new to the practice. Utilizing the act of lighting a candle or multiple candles as a visual anchor can substantially enhance your capacity to sustain focused attention. It can be quite powerful.

16. Please ensure that you do not become excessively anxious or overwhelmed. This may pose a challenge for individuals who are new to it, however, it remains the foremost crucial advice. Irrespective of any eventualities encountered during the process of meditation, it is imperative that you abstain from fixating or becoming distressed about the matter at hand. This also encompasses experiencing anxiety or apprehension in relation to the practice of meditation.

17. Kindly ensure that you are accompanied by a partner. Occasionally, individuals can derive advantages from engaging in meditation alongside a supportive group or a trusted companion. One may engage in a conversation with a close acquaintance or family member regarding the advantages of meditation and establish a collaborative effort. If there is someone who supports your endeavors and you reciprocate the support, it can evolve into a collaborative endeavor that will prove advantageous for both parties involved.

18. Engage in morning meditation. The early hours of the morning are undeniably the optimal designated period for engaging in deliberate practice. It is more tranquil, fostering a mental environment free from the usual

distractions and mental clutter of daily life. Additionally, the probability of being distracted is lower. Establish the commendable practice of rising at least thirty minutes earlier than others to engage in the practice of meditation.

19. Express gratitude for the opportunity. Once you have concluded your meditation session, allocate a few moments to cultivate a sense of gratitude for the opportunity bestowed upon you to engage in this practice, as well as for the attentiveness exhibited by your mind.

20. Pay attention if your interest starts to dwindle. Engaging in meditation can be challenging during the initial stages. There will come a juncture where it no longer aligns with the overall framework

or vision you have in mind. Kindly observe and acknowledge this matter. This is the point at which rigorous practice becomes essential.

Initially, upon commencing my meditation practice, I harbored the notion that I would be compelled to embrace an ascetic lifestyle akin to that of a monk, relinquishing indulgence in activities such as watching television and going to the cinema, along with renouncing other contemporary pleasures one encounters in daily existence. I anticipated returning home from work, making a cup of tea, igniting a candle, and peacefully contemplating the sunset through my window with a benevolent gaze.

Not a terrible idea. On occasion, perhaps even several times per week, it is beneficial to disengage from contemporary amenities and observe the impact on one's well-being. It is highly probable that initially you may experience a slight unease, but subsequently, you are likely to encounter an exquisite state of tranquility.

In conclusion, I suggest that we continue engaging in activities that bring us joy, as long as we approach them with mindful consideration. By performing these actions with conscientiousness, we can avoid excessive indulgence. This goes for absolutely everything, with media being no different.

I would suggest reducing your consumption and directing your attention towards thoroughly relishing the time you allocate to watching your preferred television program or film. This entails devoting genuine focus to the narrative, the characters, the orchestration, the hues of the costumes, the voices that resonate most profoundly, and the wonder of distant vistas. Allow yourself to become captivated, akin to your sense of wonderment as a child, when you would lose yourself in the narrative unfolding before you. Remember that feeling?

It is impossible to discern the subtle intricacies of these mystical entities while holding your mobile device. Please place it down and store it properly. Hide it. Seriously.

There is no justification for engaging in multiple tasks while we are engaged in watching television. However, we engage in this activity without pause. To what extent do we engage in purposeless phone scrolling, wherein we frequently peruse social media platforms or explore electronic retail sites, all while endeavoring to comprehend the unfolding narrative of the television program?" I must admit, I am indeed culpable of immediately reaching for my phone the moment a show or movie I am watching becomes tedious or when a commercial break ensues.

While it may not be catastrophic to have our phones in our possession while viewing a film, it is of utmost importance to uphold and enhance our concentration and cognizance as a testament of respect. Our patience. If we can't sit still and pay attention to a twenty-two minute TV show without checking our bank account, our friends' Instagram pages, eBay, and People Magazine, then how do we expect to be present with our difficult emotions?

This week, select a television show or film to view and make a deliberate effort to be fully engaged in the experience. No distractions. Please make an effort to focus and allow the creators to narrate their story to you.

Additionally, depending on your current state, it may be advantageous to moderate your speed and proceed at a more leisurely tempo. Through the practice of meditation and the cultivation of mindfulness, one will develop a heightened awareness of the rhythm of their thoughts and the movements of their body. If you have experienced an exceptionally busy day, it would be advisable to forgo watching films such as Terminator or those involving car chases. Despite any desire for diversion, it would be advisable to unwind and peruse a book this evening, affording your body the opportunity to decelerate.

*

All of these notions hold validity in the context of music as well. A composition that evokes deep emotional vulnerability or evokes profound sentiment within one's heart? Allow it to proceed in precisely that manner. Feel all those feels. I find music more captivating than even visually stimulating forms of entertainment such as on-screen media. I derive great pleasure from engaging in the act of listening to music while operating a vehicle or engaging in domestic duties, as I am able to enter a state of focused concentration. It is my experience that practicing mindfulness while listening to music feels remarkably instinctive and effortless.

Select a melody that is entirely unfamiliar to you. Pay profound attention to every rhythm and subtlety of speech, as though they encompass the utmost significance in the world at that precise instant. You may also discover a suitable musical composition to engage with during moments of unease, which you can repeatedly utilize to redirect your thoughts to the present instance, while embracing its comforting melodies.

The Chronicle of Discerning Affection

As previously outlined, we possess the tendency to pass judgement on all facets of our existence. Indeed, the level of judgment has escalated to the point where our blessings have manifested as unintended misfortunes. The detachment we experience from our fundamental emotions enables our incessantly active mind to engage in intellectualization, resulting in the formation of judgments. However, it is not possible to pass judgment or quantify emotions or feelings. They remain unchanged in their current state. I am presenting a brief anecdote highlighting our tendency to evaluate our parents without fully recognizing their shared humanity with us. How frequently we place upon them the weight of attaining flawlessness and impose upon them our lofty anticipations. We make them sit on the highest pedestal and expect them to make no mistakes whatsoever.

Furthermore, it is expected that they possess emotional, financial, and mental competence to effectively navigate all circumstances related to our needs. They must demonstrate exemplary qualities to be showcased and designated as exemplary parents within their surrounding community. All outputs originating from their end must exhibit impeccable quality.

Mani, an adolescent boy in the early stages of his teenage years, consistently regarded Raj's parents with admiration. He consistently held the belief that they embodied the epitome of exemplary guardianship, surpassing the expectations of any child. Raj's parents were well-qualified and operating a thriving enterprise, while conversely, Mani's parents originated from a rural community. His father engaged in agricultural pursuits, whereas his mother assumed the role of a domestic professional with limited academic credentials. Nevertheless, she dedicated a significant amount of time to her children and selflessly attended to their needs.

As Mani matured, he consistently criticized his mother's lack of proficiency in table etiquette and her inability to project herself appropriately. Continuing in this manner, Mani transitioned into adulthood. He made a personal commitment to marry a competent woman, and he followed through on his promise. Now arrived the moment when Mani assumed the role of a father. Following the conclusion of his wife's maternity leave, she recommenced her professional pursuits while their son was consequently entrusted to the care of a daycare facility. Over the course of several additional years, it became evident to him that his son consistently expressed dissatisfaction regarding the manner in which his friends' mothers devoted time to their children, engaging in activities such as meal preparation and evening outings to parks.

His son began expressing to him that he was indeed fortunate, as his grandmother dedicated all her time to him, carrying out tasks that his peers experience with their own mothers. One day, the son expressed, "Father, I yearn for your mother to be my mother, as it would afford me ample opportunity to express my love for her and demonstrate my deep desire to always be in her company."

This statement abruptly jarred Mani, causing him to reminisce about a past exchange with Raj wherein he expressed, "I desire that your mother was my own, for then I would idolize her."

This revelation prompted Mani to recognize the inherent perfection present in every mother, regardless of their individual attributes. It is due to the weight of our expectations that they appear flawed in our perception. This realization brought tears to his eyes as he lamented the absence of his mother in corporeal existence, denying him the ability to share this experience with her. He perceived a distinct sense of misplacement in regards to that period, which had consistently been devoted to his interactions with the maternal figure.

The aforementioned narrative holds true for a significant proportion of individuals, wherein there exists a common desire for others to embody a flawless image akin to the idealized constructs we create within our thoughts. We formulate a mental representation of their conduct, cognitions, and affective states. However, it must be acknowledged that every individual possesses inherent perfection in their unique manner. The time has come to liberate our parents from the burdens of our expectations and simultaneously emancipate ourselves. We must refrain from making judgments and instead focus on embracing life. These appraisals obscure our ability to delve beneath the superficial aspects of the circumstances and situations. It is imperative to hold in high regard all that we have been bestowed by them, as these are indeed gifts that have been bestowed upon us by them. Each individual possesses both common attributes and distinctive characteristics. We, too, are common individuals who have inherited this existence from our progenitors, much like everyone else. Therefore, since our parents are also individuals with parental responsibilities, anticipating qualities in them that they do not possess would impede our ability to benefit from their guidance and support. This is the juncture at which we commence to establish limitations in order to engage with life, or alternatively, we commence to insulate ourselves. Instead of progressing towards greater abundance in life, we begin to gravitate towards deficiency. The presence of vitality is plentiful in the natural world. To partake in this bountifulness, it is necessary for us to be receptive to the essence of LIFE emanating from our progenitors.

Our initial criterion for evaluation invariably revolves around our parents, given that they assume the role of the primary caretakers in our lives and serve as our initial point of interaction. Therefore, in order to liberate ourselves from this cyclical pattern of judging others and evaluating our own experiences, it is imperative that our primary influencers in life, specifically our parents, are emancipated from our influence. Unbeknownst to us, while engaging in the process of passing judgments upon others, we have inadvertently begun to condemn our own lives as well. The outcome entails experiencing a dearth of tranquility, affection, accomplishment, and zest for life. We all aspire to lead a life filled with inspiration. A life that exudes internal fulfillment and vitality - what are we procrastinating for? "Allow us to engage in this practice of meditation as exemplified below:

Meditation:

1. Please shut your eyes and inhale deeply a few times to cleanse your mind. Inhale through your nasal passage and exhale through your oral cavity.

2. Exhale any accumulated stress, tension, concerns, anxieties, and intrusive thoughts. Allow every exhaled breath to be a means of releasing any mental or emotional clutter, and let every inhaled breath bring forth a renewed sense of vitality and freshness.

3. Permit yourself to achieve inner serenity and equilibrium.

4. Envision your parents directly within your field of vision. Observe them as you

likely did when you were in your infancy or perhaps during your early childhood. You gazed upon them with an unconditional and nonjudgmental affection.

5. As you observe them with boundless love, take notice of the reciprocated affection and endearment that emanates from their gaze towards you. There is no judgment coming from their side too. Gaze into their eyes, observe their nurturing embrace, witness their affectionate treatment, and acknowledge their profound reverence towards your being. The manner in which your parents gaze into your eyes, survey your physique, and appraise your physical attributes, thereby experiencing a sense of profound self-satisfaction.

6. They consistently experience a sense of pride in you, as they take pride in the fact that they have welcomed you into

their lives. Experience the profound unity residing within you, comprising their affection and connection as a man and woman, as a married couple, and as parents.

7. While experiencing this sense of unity, privately affirm within your heart, "My beloved parents, you possess the attributes of ordinary and typical parents like any other." You demonstrate a profound capacity for love, care, and affectionate behavior. I deeply apologize for my misguided attempts to find flawlessness within you, which led me to impose unrealistic expectations upon you incessantly. I deeply apologize for that. I have relinquished the expectations I have imposed upon you and myself, granting both of us liberation."

8. While engaging in this activity, it is advisable to slightly lower your head as

a gesture exemplifying respect and reverence. Breathe out all the expectations you've set for them in your mind and heart.

9. Once more, internally convey the following sentiment: "Beloved mother and father, you are unquestionably the suitable guardians for me, and I am undoubtedly the fitting offspring for you." We are ideally suited to one another in all aspects."

10. While articulating your sentiments, maintain direct eye contact with them, as their eyes brim with an abundance of pure happiness and affection. Examine your own inner self and experience the profound sense of unity and interconnectedness that you experience with them.

11. You are now able to effortlessly experience the benevolent and invigorating presence of LIFE FORCE

ENERGY coursing through your being, filling you with delight. Allow the connection to flow effortlessly, fostering a deep sense of unity with your parents.

12. After sufficiently internalizing this energy and relinquishing any accompanying judgments, permit yourself to assimilate this newly acquired vitality.

13. Once you have achieved a sense of assimilation within yourself, express your gratitude to your parents, the life force energy, and the Universe. When completed, begin to gradually, softly, and composedly open your eyes.

An alternative perspective on our parents would entail viewing them through the lens of their childhood. Similar to us, they also embodied the qualities of youthful innocence, aspirations, and fervor. Due to the fact that they have bestowed upon us this existence, we have elevated them to a position of absolute reverence, wherein they are held to an impeccable standard devoid of any potential errors. It is imperative for us that they exhibit exemplary parenthood. This is the juncture at which we inadvertently overlook the utmost fundamental aspect, namely that they also possessed the innocence of childhood. In addition, they included individuals of average status, such as their parents. They embarked on their own emotionally transformative voyage and underwent distinct childhood encounters. It is plausible that they experienced unfulfilled expectations during their upbringing from their parents and primary caregivers. The following meditation invites you on a transformative voyage, allowing you to reflect upon their former selves as they navigated the journey of maturation. It is imperative that we acknowledge the fact that they did not come into this world with the inherent identity of being parents. In contrast to us, they, too, entered the world as infants exuding a sense of joy and contentment.

Tackling Fear

Fear poses as a significant impediment. It impedes your life's forward trajectory. Throughout the course of your lifetime, you may discover that you have experienced various types of apprehensions. They possess a transient nature, yet possess the potential to resurface unexpectedly, eliciting accelerated heart rates and heightened blood pressure levels. The anxious and nervous feelings that can arise, occasionally driving one to desperation, stem from the physiological reaction of one's body to the sensation of fear experienced by the mind. Nevertheless, acquiring the skill of meditation enables individuals to gain a broader understanding of their experiences and diminish their sense of apprehension. The types of matters for which it proves advantageous are as follows:

- Test anxiety
- Examination apprehension
- Nervousness towards assessments
- Apprehension of not succeeding
- Anxiety regarding potential failure
- Unease associated with the possibility of
- Reluctance towards unfamiliar experiences
- Reluctance towards alterations
- Nyctophobia
- Apprehension regarding negative judgment.

Each and every one of these fears is unquestionably genuine. In the professional setting, the introduction of a new system, especially when one is content with the existing system, tends to evoke a sense of apprehension. The apprehension arises from a lack of certainty regarding one's ability to perform competently or grasp the necessary knowledge to excel in one's professional role. The apprehension towards change bears great resemblance. It is possible that you will be relocating to an unfamiliar location where you lack acquaintances. It might not be within your discretion, but rather a decision influenced by your partner's employment circumstances. This might push you beyond your usual boundaries.

Anxieties manifest as tangible realities. One may find themselves in the obscurity of their bedroom and perceive sounds, which are merely the routine creaks of an aged dwelling. Within the confines of your thoughts, there exists a possibility of peril concealing itself within every nook and cranny. You are not alone, and if you succumb to fear, it can greatly impede your progress. Nevertheless, meditation has a profound tendency to instill serenity within individuals, cultivating an enhanced capacity to embrace and adapt to any circumstance that may arise in life. It can assist individuals struggling with aviophobia to conquer their fear.

How meditation enables the substitution of fear

Through the practice of meditation, one acquires the ability to regulate one's breath in a particular manner. Hence, when encumbered by fear, one can anticipate that it will induce a respiration pattern that is deleterious to one's well-being. You hyperventilate. Meditation instructs individuals in replacing such a reaction with a considerably more rational approach, employing meditative techniques to cultivate a state of enhanced tranquility. In the context of an airplane, for instance, one would occupy their designated seat and gently shut one's eyes. You are undoubtedly aware that your apprehension towards air travel is unfounded, yet you struggle to manage it. Upon acquiring the skill of meditation, one gains the ability to shut out the external world by closing one's eyes, directing focus towards the breath, and consequently, swapping fear for a palpable sense of tranquility by virtually transporting oneself to an alternate realm. Consequently, upon the aircraft's departure, one is not privy to the audible propulsion emanating from the engines. Meditation serves as a means of soothing oneself, working by effectively eradicating any space within the mind for the harboring of fears. It would be highly recommended for a student who feels anxious about an upcoming examination to engage in meditation prior to the test. After completing all the preparatory work, it is inconsequential to fret, although certain students persist in doing so. The apprehension surrounding the examination environment hinders individuals from performing optimally, as their mental capacity becomes overwhelmed by the various components contributing to this fear, leading to errors. Nevertheless, by practicing meditation before the examination, the student can approach the task with a serene mindset, unfettered by negative thoughts that impede their cognitive faculties required for successfully addressing the questions at hand.

How many interviews did you attempt to complete while being hindered by a prevailing sense of apprehension? Anxiety is perceptible to those around us. You exhibit visible signs of nervousness, provide incorrect responses, and reflect upon missed opportunities to truly showcase your genuine self to the interviewers. Engaging in pre-interview meditation aids in cultivating a state of tranquility, enabling one to navigate the interview process with ease while also attaining clarity regarding one's identity and career aspirations within the position at hand.

Despite the inhibiting nature of fears, the practice of meditation serves as an effective tool for mitigating their impact. If one considers the mind as comprising various compartments, overburdening them with emotional issues, thoughts of defeat, and negative emotions like anger and jealousy impedes the proper functioning of the mind. There exists a conspicuous absence of room for creative expression and positive ideation. In the absence of such a positive mindset, your pessimism impedes your progression in life or places a hindrance on your ability to embark on new opportunities. Indeed, the stepping stone is imperceptible as all that is visible to you are the myriad issues. Fear diminishes all of the potential inherent in your life.

I recollect my sister, who exemplified exemplary behavior, confiding in me about her feelings of envy towards me. That astonished me given her consistent ranking as the top student in class and her seemingly perpetual ability to maintain a well-organized life. Subsequently, I came to the realization of the absent component. She harbored genuine apprehension towards life. She adhered to a consistent trajectory that prevented her from truly relaxing and enjoying herself. Her life comprised a sequence of triumphs, albeit ones that were secure and readily attainable for her. She had never acquired the ability to derive genuine pleasure from life the way I had. When I shared my philosophy with her, she eagerly embraced it, as her apprehension stemmed from an aversion towards enjoyment, adventure, and anything that fell beyond the confines of the beliefs ingrained in her by my parents.

All individuals possess the ability to relinquish their fears. Meditation facilitates the cultivation of a tranquil state of mind, thereby removing any mental obstacles that impede the process of experimentation. It judges no one. It resides in the present moment. It does not carry the burden of past emotional baggage nor concern itself with the uncertainties of tomorrow. Meditation is centered on embracing the present moment, recognizing its significance in the temporal dimension. Once this understanding is internalized and integrated into one's lifestyle, apprehensions dissipate, enabling individuals to embark on a fulfilling journey towards their aspirations, unimpeded by chronic disillusionment. At that juncture, apprehension recedes into the background. This is the point at which you discern the individual in control of steering the direction of your life.

www.ingramcontent.com/pod-product-compliance
Lightning Source LLC
Chambersburg PA
CBHW050236120526
44590CB00016B/2108